WORD DANCING

poems, prose and art

Jeanne Powell

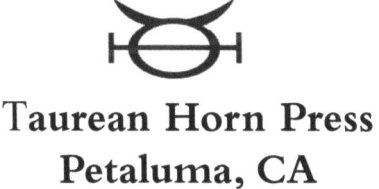

Taurean Horn Press
Petaluma, CA

copyright © 2016 by Jeanne Powell
http://jeanne-powell.com

ALL RIGHTS RESERVED

No part of this book may be reproduced or transmitted in any form or by any means, electronic or mechanical, including photocopying, recording, or by any information storage and retrieval system, without permission
in writing from the author.

published by
Taurean Horn Press, Petaluma, California

Printed in 2016

ISBN 978-0-931552-20-5

drawing on page 137 by Mimi Stuart
21 collages © Jeanne Powell
cover photograph © Jeanne Powell

Purchase from
local booksellers
or online.

ACKNOWLEDGEMENTS

"Journey" in SACRED GROUNDS ANTHOLOGY #8, Minotaur Press, Oakland, CA, 2001.

"East Bay Miracle" in DRUMVOICES REVUE tenth anniversary issue, vol. 11, nos. 1 & 2, Southern Illinois University at Edwardsville, 2003.

"Ordinary People" and "Sunset Bar" appeared in MY OWN SILENCE from Meridien PressWorks, 2006.

"Swing Dance", "When I Was" and "Reflecting" appeared in WINDOWS & SKYLIGHTS anthology, Benicia First Tuesday Poets, Outskirts Press, 2010.

Contents:

NEW POEMS	1
Reflecting	2
Looking Homeward	3
When I Was	4
Without a Map	5
Swing Dance	7
What Do You Lack?	8
When It Rains	9
Don't Tell Me I Can't Rhyme	10
The Toll It Takes	11
Passing Through Her Bedroom	12
Pocahontas	13
About Time	14
There Are Nights	15
Endless Longing [Li Po]	16
Dark Matters	17
Five Minute Warning	18
Lazy Susan	19
Old Man with Beard	20
Stop the Loss	22
About That Woman	25
SELECTED PROSE	49
Ordinary People	51
Sunset Bar	52
Camilla and Albert	54
Something About Lorena	56
When Christmas Comes Around	59
Darkrooms of My Heart	62
Coconut Cake	64
SELECTED POETRY	65
FROM FEBRUARY VOICES [1994]	67
A Poet at 79	69
Flashback	70
Meditation (1987-1989)	71
Madre	72

East Bay Miracle	73
Memoir	75
Games	76
Damage Control	77
Dempsey	78
Summer School 1991	80
Triage	81
Winnie Mandela	82
Neighbors	83
Night Crawlers	84
FROM CADENCES [1996]	105
Affirmation	107
Autumn Revisited	108
Experiencing Technical Difficulties	110
In the Shadow of the bridge	111
January—In the Rain	112
Journey	113
Running Wild	114
Souvenirs	116
Street Music	118
FROM TANGERINE DANCE [1999]	121
The Assassin	123
Tangerine	124
Saint Thomas on Hyde Street	125
Seeing Miss Rosa (1997)	126
Keeping Watch	127
Haikus	129
I Looked for You in a Mayonnaise Jar	133
A Trace of Honey	134
The Shadow Knows	135

New Poems

Reflecting

let me start over
i like everything about him

he hurls impatience at men friends
down on their luck who hide out
too long on his living room floor

he caresses a serpentine cat
who guards the steep winding staircase
to his private world

he laughs about the train wrecks
littering his love life

he makes minestrone from scratch
the way his grandmother taught

he stretches nice and slow
filling a doorway without making a sound

he caresses a guitar before rippling its strings
into soundblasts of anger

he waits free of time and judgment
for the old scars of a new friend to heal

he is a nurturing silence
with saki at sunset

let me start over
i like everything about him

© 2016 Jeanne Powell

Looking Homeward

If I were queen again
I would resurrect the ancient state of Lydia
and lecture its famous king about the treacherous future of money
so he could coin another kind of currency for his realm.

If I were queen again
I would offer greater service to the Mother of us all
that She might show mercy to Her lost children
and welcome them back to the garden of eden.

If I were queen again
I would declare it a cardinal sin
requiring banishment from this earthly plane
to compromise the childhood of any living thing.

When I am queen again
it will be as it was, as the Mother decreed 7,000 years ago
the lion shall lie down with the lamb and the fox with the hen
when I am queen again, all will be well forever.

© 2016 Jeanne Powell

When I Was

When
I was
just a girl
parents
invariably commanded
me to be
quiet,
more "still,"
free of freedom
because
childhood requires
training, sacrifice, breaking.
Notice
news is
"breaking news" today,
have
you witnessed
this phenomenal, mad
phrasing?
People believing –
as they must –
that
broken is
the perfect way.

Without a Map

Sometimes you undertake long journeys
without a map, without a calendar,
without even a clock
because you know it's time.
A voice deep inside urges,
an attic door creaks open and
you catch a glimpse of forgotten light
and wistful eyes.
You hear the ticking of hours you
would rather not count
and sense the face of a time piece
you cannot fathom or see.

You know you're searching for a
trunk, navy blue, last seen
in a small sunlit corner of your
grandmother's front parlor,
on a polished hardwood floor
near a bookcase painted white
and a window facing peach trees.

You're searching for the reason Sister chose
not to advise you Nana was on her deathbed,
the reason you chose to go underground,
the reason Mother never talked about Nana,
or the reason Mother never spoke
about anything at all.

© 2016 Jeanne Powell

You're hoping for a chance to replay the tape
that Akashic record of all you say or do or feel.
This time all will come out differently.
Sister may call you, Mother may still be there,
Nana may live until you arrive
by plane and taxi and design.

And the trunk, wonderful and magical,
brimming with memories and treasures,
surrounded by leather bound Scriptures
and other cautionary tales
remains locked and in waiting
until you remove the carpet and insert the key
and bring possibility alive again.

© 2016 Jeanne Powell

SWING DANCE
(for my mother)

When you left me to go hide
in that silk-lined casket
I pulled fresh dandelions
and hid them in my coat
until the grave diggers
rested their shovels.
I scattered your lioness dandies
on the dirt covering your new home.
Near the end of my childish days
you always did travel without me.
This cemetery trick was no new game.

To see you dance once more
to that swing music you liked on the radio
when you thought no one was watching
recalling a time before husband
and kids and worries
when you worked swing shift
with all the other Rosies
then danced the night away.
To hear you laugh once more
would have been sweet.

© 2016 Jeanne Powell

What Do You Lack?

What do you lack
Lady
what do you lack?

Queen Anne's lace
sharpened knives
blood oranges
a few good times
old bell towers
and rusty chimes

what do you lack
Lady
what do you lack?

When It Rains

Rain patter, rain chatter
sit 'em down
and what's the matter

dad dead, mother dying
what's the use
of so much crying
cry a little, cry a lot
circumstances we begot
dance and chant
scream and rant
so clearly was their dismal ending
written before time forgot

rain patter, rain chatter
sit 'em down
and what's the matter

© 2016 Jeanne Powell

Don't Tell Me I Can't Rhyme

I would never tell you
that you're unable to rhyme
or not allowed to rhyme
that rhyming can be
hazardous to your health
brought down an empire
or built a brave new world

I would never tell you
that rhyming brings laughter
to a child in the park
or a smile to a mariner's face
on a cold wet night.

I will tell you that rhyme
knows even in its absence
that rhyme believes
in the present and hereafter
that rhyme, by loving design,
is

© 2016 Jeanne Powell

The Toll It Takes

Relaxed in sweet William's Thunderbird
riding high on poetry
we approach the Golden Gate
where the ferryman stands guard

backseat Barbi brings forth a five $ bill
unprecedented for her
but trusty William knows the toll
is always ready to pay

pay the toll for another, I said
a random act of kindness
no, I won't, she replied
but you already offered, I said
do it for beauty, I sighed
she refused, I know, because I said

so we crossed that other bridge
when we got to it
the silence clashing around us
leaving the toll for another unpaid
isn't it always this way,
and why? I say

© 2016 Jeanne Powell

Passing Through Her Bedroom

Hiking boots her only pillow
she sleeps on the harsh sidewalk
near my front steps

Her stocking feet shiver
struggle to stay within the folds
of a single blanket

Does she dream
surrounded by pillow clouds
on sheets of sunlight?

Am I the only one who shuts down
the cell phone and walks softly
when passing through her bedroom?

© 2016 Jeanne Powell

Pocahontas

Epitaph
discovered
recently
for a prisoner of war
long forgotten

captured princess
summersaulting
between manicured
hedges guarding
an English estate

discarded wild-wife
initiated evasive action
against the burden
of interlopers hunting
a new world to plunder

leaving
her name
written in blood
forever
between two lands

© 2016 Jeanne Powell

About Time

Seems like I'm running out of time
the world is ready to rumble
showcasing weapons cataclysmic
inmates are running the asylum
lost time when I was Sleeping Beauty
and when I chased a tardy rabbit
through those looking-glass doors

seems like I'm running out of time
my one true prince is tied up
in a colossal traffic jam
on the twilight side of Malta
billboards selling Soylent Green
dominate the grimy landscape
texting outpaces the Scriptures
my boots ran over their heels
the wind is blowing down my door
too many paces behind

seems like I'm running out of time

© 2016 Jeanne Powell

There Are Nights

My hair is shoulder length again
and I laugh, tossing dark locks
as you nibble each cinnamon toe
even the ones without nails

when I feel shy before sunset, you gather me
and place me gently on the closet floor
before lifting my hips
from the red coral carpet

nights when I say no, Aunt Flo is in town
the red river is over its banks
you just chuckle and pull my string
then settle in for a long slow swim

My sturdy kitchen table is set for one
leaving room for you to place me on it
knees akimbo
while you sit and dine with gusto

these days
there are nights
that just don't
ever seem to happen

© 2016 Jeanne Powell

Endless Longing [Li Po]

I

Together
such words we spoke
memories of Chang-an
breathed into our skin, our flesh.
Golden light bathed us through open curtains.
Sounds of autumn chirped a warning
at our well of happiness.
Even as we drew close together at night
light frost formed a bleak rim around our mat.
Lamp light leaked away and deserted to the moon
leaving futility in its wick.
Soon your rose petals divided and reformed
beyond the edges of clouds,
beauty now above me and far away.
My thoughts rippled through
waves of bitter longing above and below
tears from my dream soul.

II

Burnt offerings
our flowering lies in embers under a moon bright and sad.
I am a phoenix rising now, searching for my music man.
My lute leans on a hardwood column, longs for favor and fidelity.
In the past, sweet harmony. Where is my music man?
Our strings attuned, we played in pairs, Mandarin duck and drake.
Now a spring wind blows and plucky swallows struggle
to carry my tears toward a blue sky.
So far away, too far, my love.
Our past falters, falls back, shadows mirror longings.
I am broken in the wrenching
come back
I am broken.

© 2016 Jeanne Powell

Dark Matters

My shadow
isn't mine anymore
it splits atoms
alters molecules
neutralizes expectations

the fear
is about more
than my shadow
it's about the dark
remember
we all are afraid
of the dark now
such a long time between suns

dark matters
shroud us
in spider webs of worry
it's what we have become
radioactive
half-eaten
just desserts

© 2016 Jeanne Powell

Five Minute Warning

I had power once
last Tuesday, the sixteenth

took all your fancy clothing
from the laundry hamper
basement trunk and upstairs closet
piled it all in the front seat
of your shiny new Pontiac truck
poured gasoline from your tank
and lit it up with an eight-inch handpainted
fireplace match from Pottery Barn

You could see the flames for miles and miles
I didn't have a choice really
you disregarded my five-minute warning
more than once

© 2016 Jeanne Powell

Lazy Susan

I saw you leaving tonight
with the surly foreign wench

Buried behind mounds
of dirty dishes, I surfaced long enough
to see you two slide
into your favorite Mercedes

Her fire-engine lips
pulled on your Egyptian cigarette
and she grazed your skin
with her glossy nails

When I finish these dishes
and close the cafe tonight,
I plan to sit up late
in the humid dark and wait

I'll have a kitchen blade
in my hand when you come back
for more cash, the way you do

And then we'll talk
it's time

© 2016 Jeanne Powell

Old Man with Beard

I see you everywhere, on currency we trust, on the covers of official histories, in portraits of God.

Midnight silhouettes of you standing on the broken spines of my ancestors have haunted me all my days.

Each day you occupy iron benches in the city parks with lemon-peel smiles and that sliver of hardness glinting under blue-veined lids.

In every town you take back lunch counters, Clorox public schools, hide a nation's skeletons in frostbitten beards and gnarled hands.

I know who you were, before you started eating prunes and voiding through a tube.

You used to hang out in turpentine woods, along dark back roads, near pitiless swamps with a knife to gut, a rope to hang and an axe to grind.

You know I know where you've been, you know I know what you did, know every time you wash your hands, the falling water runs red.

The only thing you have to do is outlive your enemies, right? Assassinate the leaders you fear, let them see the promised land early on, before too many see their greatness here.

You need only wait for citizens to follow their ordinary ways, plod from minute to hour, overwhelmed by regrets and your stark display of power.

© 2016 Jeanne Powell

Your time is coming because witnesses grow frail, don't want you on their conscience their last moments in this vale.

The lonesome death of Hattie Carroll, gentle wife Viola Liuzzo, four little girls on Birmingham Sunday - Denise McNair, Addie Mae Collins, Cynthia Wesley, Carole Robertson.

You know I know where you've been, you know I know what you did, know every time you wash your hands, the falling water runs red.

© 2016 Jeanne Powell

Stop the Loss

ONE:
Rumors of war, we're at it again,
only the 20th time since I came of age.
civilian bodies litter foreign boulevards,
American coffins fill airport corners.
we watch with resignation as reservists go off to die.
involunteers, unaware of stop loss,
and other sly devices utilized
to keep them at the front forever.

Now the women are dying, American women,
along with thousands of civilian fatalities
consecrating battlefields in Afghanistan,
a land so ancient that time has forgotten.
I never thought we would let that happen,
you and I, yes you, you're the ones I'm speaking to.
easy to overlook the loss of women
unless you see through patriotic headlines
into underfinanced corners
of your tv screen at 2:00 o'clock in the morning.

Look closely at photographs ending
the News Hour on PBS, and you'll see
lipstick traces and locks of hair under
military headgear, with names like
Emma and Maria, confronting you in silence,
that's how you tell.
of course, you only see those photos
after they die and next of kin are notified.

© 2016 Jeanne Powell

What did they hope to achieve, these women?
to serve well and support their families.
you read about the Native American marine,
single mother on a reservation
whose death so far away left two children
with only grandparents to care.

you know that earnest carpenter on cable,
who gives away houses to families in crisis?
he and his crew built a strong new house
for survivors of the dead reservist,
two bewildered elders raising orphans forever wounded
by the loss they were powerless to stop.

TWO:
You watch the 6:00 o'clock news
with one eye open and an ear half-cocked
while you multi-task in your busy life.
the war again, edited to fit your tv screen.
a high-pitched wailing scream,
then medics load an American fighter
into an ambulance, cameras avoiding her face,
while the journalist, embedded, drones on and on.
clearly, we must not know about her death before her parents.

Only this one didn't die. they shipped her
to Germany, then home to the VA.
Germany called MASH in Iraq asking,
why did you send her? you know she won't make it.
they answered back, wait and see,
this one will surprise you.
such a long battle she faced at home,
just a reservist getting second-class care,
but doctors and family fought the system.
somehow she got what was needed to survive.

© 2016 Jeanne Powell

Her brain kept on swelling,
so doctors removed part of her skull,
stored it inside her good leg for safe-keeping.
months of PT for the leg that was shattered,
fighting through pain, surgery, more pain.
she did not recognize anyone from before,
not even the man who visited each day.
hospital staff fell in love with her courage.

Stateside called Germany and MASH in Iraq,
see how she's doing, she made it, come see.
one day she remembered who she was,
remembered the man who never left her side.
by the date of the wedding, she was walking with a cane.
she kept both legs, and her skull was intact.
a hard-fought, hard-won bittersweet ending.

If only we could stop the loss,
enforce a ban on undeclared wars,
raise the enlistment age to 30,
draft the old before the young,
hold the president accountable,
find the courage to fight for these women and all the others.

★

[paragraph 9c of the enlistment contract states:
in the event of war, enlistment in the Armed Forces
continues until six (6) months after the war ends…]

© 2016 Jeanne Powell

About That Woman

I

Remember that time, long ago and far away
yesterday and still today
there was this woman
she harvested crops after planting and tending the seeds
she wove cloth from yarn she spun, and made clothes by hand
that woman carried the burden of seed
implanted for nine full months
gave birth on her knees over a blanket of leaves
gave birth on a dirt floor, or under a tree
by the shores of a raging river too dangerous to cross
gave birth in a desert oasis at night
gave birth on the fields of war as well as peace
gave birth when hope was alive
and during winter's frozen fears.

that woman gave birth to art painted on walls while
stranded in ancient caves with children
gave birth to clever traps for hunting Stone Age prey
wielded a club to keep masculine predators at bay
that woman carried grief as gamely
as she carried her offspring and tools and male violence
until she could discern a better way

she wore woven skirts in rain forests
long dresses in temples of the Gods
fur pelts in northern winters
and nothing at all on islands deep in the Pacific womb
until belief in a solitary male god
dressed this woman in shrouds of pain
pain she wore as a scourge from another world
deprived of her birthright, she stormwalked
through the blood of women already sacrificed.

© 2016 Jeanne Powell

that woman, any woman, every woman
she was 14 and sold into slavery
she was 16 and fought on ancient battlefields
she was 20 and worked as a blacksmith
she was 30 and burned at the stake
she was 40 and revered as a wise one
she was 50 alone and homeless
she was 60 and ran for president

II
wait they said
it's not your time yet
you're 51% of the world
some strange wisdom of Nature
but we still need to burn you
on your husband's political pyre
still need to pay you 79 cents to every dollar he makes
make you give birth at our pleasure and not yours
use your body to sell every product on the market
keep you as our punching bag
both at home and in the public square, they said

college graduate, advocate, wife, mother, taxpayer, counselor,
survivor of the marriage wars,
goodwill ambassador, member of the august senate,
you wait, girl, it's not your turn,
don't you make trouble now,
just drop out, remember your place

© 2016 Jeanne Powell

that woman who scrubs floors, who farms, who fights in wars,
works construction, waits on tables, lives on scraps,
builds a nation with her blood and sweat, survives rape,
nurtures children through it all,
forgives her captors, survives the death of hope,
century after century for 5,000 years

    wait, they say, again and forever
    but we must not let that happen
    for when and where we enter
    the whole world enters with us

★★★

© 2016 Jeanne Powell

© 2016 Jeanne Powell

© 2016 Jeanne Powell

© 2016 Jeanne Powell

Selected Prose

© 2016 Jeanne Powell

Ordinary People

That first year in my town's only secondary school, I realized something was different about my family. There was no summer cottage on the lake for us, no graceful sailboat at the end of the pier. We did not winter anywhere except the same clapboard house where I was born and raised. Dandelions brightened our crabgrass parcel in the spring, fireflies lit three-leafed clovers every summer, falling leaves decorated our weathered porch late in autumn, a full panoply of snowflakes danced on the ramshackle roof when winter came. There was nothing gourmet about Dicers Market where my mother shopped, nothing grand about fresh goat roasting on a spit near my father's union hall every Fourth of July.

Years passed and from the four corners of the earth we returned to our town with two separate bridges to a foreign country. Class reunion. Over aperitifs and hors d'oeuvres I watched and listened, my yearbook memories forever colored by this new education. There are worse things than threadbare carpets and empty cupboards, worse things than powdered eggs reconstituted on Easter morning, worse things than Salvation Army baskets on porches Christmas Eve.

You know those glass-paneled homes on Amber Lane and Azure Cove? My glittering classmates spoke of fathers in the wrong bedroom after dark. They spoke of expensive whiskey bottles empty too often, suicide dreams from which no one woke, and scarlet letters in the afterglow.

I won't throw stones, but I wish someone had for the people I used to know.

© 2016 Jeanne Powell

Sunset Bar

Late one autumn Saturday we were sitting on a plump sofa in a Sunset bar David had chosen, positioned nicely in front of the woodburning fireplace, about to snuggle, when a man and woman walked through the double doors. At first I barely noticed but they paused, longer than necessary, to survey the candlelit room and choose where they would sit. Eventually I turned my attention from the always mysterious David, and gazed at them.

You could say she was the color of chestnuts roasting on an open fire, as David once described me, but there the similarity ended. Her makeup was noticeable, as were the years she tried to hide, not so much the years, but their impact on her. The man was a bit unsteady on his feet at this hour, but amiable and familiar in his attentiveness. What drew my attention was the way she seemed to freeze when she caught sight of me.

David made a rare comment not in response to anything I had said, and I encouraged him with a dazzling smile, my dark curly hair tumbling around my bare shoulders. The couple still stood just inside the swinging doors, while the woman looked at me, stared as though she had no other choice. I checked to see if I knew her, but realized I did not.

A crackling log flared in the fireplace; I saw her clearly then and she observed me. The woman's jaw seemed to sag and slow tears glistened in bloodshot eyes. David was telling me how he discovered this pub right after returning from Ireland, while his eyes narrowed and flicked over the woman in turmoil and the ruddy drunk whose arm was comfortably around her shoulder, "Wassa matter, babe? Don't you like this place anymore? Where you wanna sit?"

© 2016 Jeanne Powell

The man chose a table nearby and with elaborate gestures held a chair for his companion. He lit a Marlboro for her. A barmaid approached and took their order. The woman's eyes never left me. Full in the moment of my joyous youth and David's sober courtship, I shrugged away her February face.

Part of me knew this was not about me or the Sunset bar. Part of me stood away, near the fireplace mantle and observed a phenomenon, that of time, which takes on everyone, like James Brown said in a song lyric. I was young and strong, and no Samson had cut my long hair. So there was time still, you see.

© 2016 Jeanne Powell

Camilla and Albert

The first year of her marriage, Camilla knew that nothing in life would be the same. Of that, she was absolutely certain. After all, she spoke in couplets now and traveled in twos. There was a familiar face to hold her chair at table and to open doors. He laughed at her witticisms and held her close at night. Conversations began with "we" instead of "I," and plans were constructed around "us" and "our." She would learn to dance as he did, and he had eyes only for her.

Adjustments had to be made. Cartons of beer now crammed refrigerator shelves in case his guy friends dropped in for football games or baseball afternoons or women's volleyball on cable. Long guns filled a corner of the hall closet. At her request, Albert stored ammunition apart from rifles and shotguns. And Camilla learned to play strip poker in front of their fireplace.

Even during those first summer months together, the bride felt a sense of snow, inhaled a hint of colder climes as she listened to his life experience. She was aware that he grew up in rural Alabama, the youngest of eight brothers and sisters. 'If you wanted meat on the table," Albert was fond of saying, "you had to hunt it, fish it or trap it." It would be months before Camilla found out about the midnight chase through stubbled fields, when Albert's father pursued his mother with an axe. Her incessant bible reading rankled the old man's nerves, Albert said. Eventually the father took up with a younger woman downriver, and was never seen again. Albert's mother returned to her Old and New Testaments, greatly relieved.

Evening meals for Camilla could be unpredictable during hunting season. Her husband awoke early on hunting weekends, placed guns in the back of his Porsche and drove to a buddy's house.

© 2016 Jeanne Powell

They loaded up and went wherever guys go, to hillsides or valleys or marshes, and brought down small birds in season, rarely missing their aim. Dead prey was cleaned and dressed at Mack and Shirley's house, or Bob and Sharon's place, then brought home for Albert to cook. Camilla stayed away from her kitchen until Albert had completed meal preparations. She pretended she was waiting for dinner in a newly discovered French bistro. She was impressed by Albert's presentation of pheasant stuffed with wild rice dressing, accompanied by cornbread baked in a heart-shaped pan and topped with honey from a local hive.

Social evenings with her husband's friends were challenging. Albert and his buddies came from the same country town. The women in their lives had interests very different from hers. She wrote sacred erotica, tracked down antiques in Benicia and loved to study ancient history. Shirley operated a hair salon and rode dirt bikes on weekends. Sharon dispatched for 911 emergency services and spent her spare time knitting and crocheting. These two couples would enter the home she shared with Albert and separate instantly, by gender, to opposite corners of the living room. Camilla had never seen anything like it.

By Christmas of their first year together, Camilla knew the marriage was struggling, was over actually, and likely to be buried in an avalanche of frozen hopes and expectations. It was a terrible time to leave Albert, this season awash in mistletoe and holly, hearty cheer and warm eggnog, mounting bills and waning joy. But Camilla's sense of cold had become overwhelming, freezing out tolerance, and hope.

© 2016 Jeanne Powell

Something About Lorena

Whenever I think about Lorena, I envision her as a puzzle wrapped in a portable maze. And I wonder whether her existence on the periphery of my life is a metaphor for what I don't know or never knew about the mango wildness lurking in women of a certain age.

Lorena comes from a charmingly dysfunctional family in the Potrero Hill district of my town. Her older sister invited me to join their family for Christmas dinner in wine country about five years ago. Two of Chrissa's three ex-husbands were present, along with assorted teens from various relationships. In this family embrace, Lorena was smooth and nurturing, the perfect attentive sister and host.

Back in the City of Oakland after the holidays, cruising in her vintage silver Mercedes and practicing her newly acquired Arabic, Lorena was anything but smooth and easygoing. Anglo-Saxon expletives filled the car, competing with Smokey Robinson for air space, as she complained about her tenants in the Visitation Valley property she owned. And she was pressing her third union grievance against the school district for trying to transfer her to another grade in a different school, again.

"I'll be damned if I'll let them get away with handing my job to some bilingual wench with half my seniority! Nearly 25 years with these bastards and they're still trying to push me around. Fascist scum! Can't wait to retire!"

What I knew, and what the school district did not know is that Lorena has a second career. She part-times as "Hot Lips" with an explicit phone service. Lorena comes home after teaching her fifth graders, puts down her bifocals, kicks off her granny shoes, ditches the girdle and plops her ample frame on the upholstered love seat in her living room. Then she calls the hotline.

© 2016 Jeanne Powell

"Hi, this is Hot Lips, and I want to work for a couple of hours." For the next 120 minutes Lorena talks and moans, giggles and pants for buttoned-down males sitting at desks in highrise buildings, their hands gripping Visas and Mastercards, except of course, when they need their hands for other purposes. In two hours she makes more money than she earns teaching all day.

Then there was the summer morning she telephoned and invited me to lunch at her duplex the next day, to see her new redwood deck. That following day, with its simple lunch of sandwiches and soup, will remain with me for a long time. Lorena met me at the BART transit station in her Mercedes. "Your car looks different," I said. "Oh, I bought a new one," she said. "So you traded in the other Mercedes?" "No, I still have the first one."

After parking in her driveway and pausing to speak to her downstairs tenant, Lorena led the way to her home upstairs. Panoramic views from her new redwood deck were breathtaking, well worth the visit. I wandered through her home taking in family photos, oil paintings on the walls, leather-bound books, and antique furniture while she made a couple of quick phone calls. "Are you about to 'go to work'?" I pantomimed. She shook her head in the negative, then hung up the phone. "The guys who built the deck for me are coming over; I still have to pay them."

We were looking at photos of her last vacation in Mexico when the door bell rang 15 minutes later. Two handsome young men bounded up the stairs and entered, very much at ease in the house. Each wore clean construction coveralls with no shirt. After Lorena introduced Mark and Joseph, I continued wandering through the house, ending up in the kitchen. After all, she needed to talk to them about the redwood deck, I reasoned. I couldn't help noticing how muscular yet graceful they were, with perfect manners.

© 2016 Jeanne Powell

Mark was blond with piercing blue eyes. Joseph was a brunette with dark brown eyes and a gold ring in one ear. Both spent a lot of time in the sun, due to their work. Mark seemed to wander into the kitchen at some point, and chatted easily with me as we looked at tea canisters and other items Lorena had placed on the table in anticipation of lunch. After a few minutes of conversation, during which I was surprisingly shy, Mark gracefully excused himself. Suddenly Joseph was there, leaning against the door frame. He also had an ease of speech and movement unusual and impressive in someone his age. Both made positive eye contact, warm and friendly and open.

I could not help wishing I were still in my twenties, and bolder than I ever had been, so I could give myself permission to notice these beautiful young construction workers. Again I marveled at how attentive they were. "How well raised they are," I thought, "and what good manners. I hope Lorena was nice to them."

Soon Mark and Joseph left the house, as discreetly as they had entered. "All finished with the guys who built your deck?" I inquired brightly as I re-entered the room where Lorena sat. With bifocals perched at the end of her nose, Lorena glowered as though she wanted to deck me right then and there. God, I knew she was moody, but what have I done now?

Lorena and I ate split pea soup and roast beef sandwiches in silence, sitting in her sunlit kitchen. She decided not to brew a pot of tea, and abruptly dropped me off at the BART station. Back in San Francisco, I pondered her strange behavior. It was a week or two before I figured it out. Lorena never invited me to lunch at her home with a view again. She sends a greeting card at Christmas, now and then. And I think a lot about that hardwood deck.

© 2016 Jeanne Powell

When Christmas Comes Around

Shimanski adjusted the wool scarf around his neck and stepped back into the wooden shelter he used as an office this time of year. Snowflakes were falling and so was the temperature but he was content. Business was good. Evergreens and pines had been moving off the tree lot with regularity, promising a profitable season. After tonight, he would close for the holidays.

His wife and sisters-in-law had spent all week cleaning and cooking. Grandparents and grandkids and in-laws filled the entire block where Shimanski lived. His brothers had bought houses nearby as soon as they returned from the war in Korea. Life was good.

Except for the colored. "Jeez, they were pushy." World War II had brought them to Detroit when the auto plants converted to war production, rolling tanks and airplane parts off the assembly lines. They were let into the union and now the colored were getting the same pay as his brothers. That didn't seem right. Everyone he knew thought they would go back south after the U.S. dropped the bomb on Japan, but that didn't happen. Something called the Cold War got going, then Korea heated up. "Now we're stuck with them," he sighed.

A few more sales of evergreens, carefully tied to Fords, Chevrolets and Buicks. Last minute purchases when people gritted their teeth and realized they couldn't face Christmas or their families without a tree.

Across the boulevard Shimanski spied a dark-skinned man, short and wiry, holding the hand of a little girl. About 30 minutes they stood there, the child as motionless as her father. He looked for their car or truck, but didn't see one parked nearby. "How the devil did they get way out here?" he wondered.

© 2016 Jeanne Powell

Finally they crossed the boulevard and approached the lot without making a sound. The men measured each other without direct eye contact. The little girl's eyes sparkled as she looked around the tree lot. "Your kid?"

"Got three more at home. Had a job out here today. Put up some shelves and fixed windows. Got paid cash. If I wait till I get home, tree lots'll be closed. Will you sell to me?"

Shimanski hesitated. "I won't come on your property. You can put the tree on the sidewalk here if you want," said the man, as still as a statue.

"I got the makings of a cart here. After we tie down the tree, we can walk OK. My kid, she's used to walking. Won't be no trouble."

Shimanski noticed the man's distinctive work clothes. Reminded him of his brother Walter, the one who had served in the Merchant Marines. Maybe this guy had too. Walter said there were colored on some ships.

He looked up and down the boulevard, then glanced at his watch. No more cars likely to pull up this time of evening. Most had driven home to put up the tree, add holiday decorations, and settle in for Christmas Eve dinner.

"I won't come on your property. You can put it on the sidewalk if you want." The man repeated quietly, and Shimanski cleared his throat, which he always did after making a decision.

"Yeah, sure, OK. Pick from over there," and he gestured toward a far corner of the tree lot. The little girl's eyes lit up. Affected somehow by the child's obvious delight, Shimanski cleared his throat again and said, "Pick from any place on the lot."

© 2016 Jeanne Powell

The mariner stepped over the property line cautiously and picked an evergreen just tall enough to fit the makeshift wagon.

"Nah, you'll need something bigger for the whole family. You said kids, right?"

"But I can't carry..."

"Don't worry. I'll drop you off. It's on my way. You live on the east side of town, right?"

Shimanski never knew what made him volunteer to drive the man and his daughter to the east side. Maybe his feet were cold and he just wanted to complete business for the night and lock up. Maybe he had too many trees left on the lot. Maybe his brother's stories about mariners' bravery during the War came back to him. Whatever it was, Shimanski had made a decision and was unstoppable after that.

The mariner, his little girl and a fairly large evergreen tree all went into the back of Shimanski's truck, and proceeded to the other side of the city. Once they reached a snowladen street of small wooden houses, the mariner had no trouble removing the tree. Shimanski stayed in the cab of his truck with the door closed.

As Shimanski drove away, the mariner stood straight and still, watching. His little daughter waved, snowflakes dancing in her long dark braids.

© 2016 Jeanne Powell

Darkrooms of My Heart

Valerie rarely cried. Few moments in life required such effort, and crying really involved a struggle. Letting go of one's emotions in front of others was unlikely to lead to any worthwhile victory and seldom even a satisfactory stalemate. Then there was the problem with eye liner, mascara and pancake makeup. Pancake always dissolved in streaks when tears flowed. She really needed to switch to loose powder.

For the third time that weekend before the presidential election, she received a telephone call from her mother. Candy was on a tear because she had discovered her latest boyfriend in the downstairs closet with the upstairs maid. Valerie was the oldest and most reliable of her five adult kids and Candy always called her when things went wrong. Things had been going wrong a lot lately.

"When I found him and brought him to my new townhouse, he was pounding rusty nails into abandoned bricks, that's how down and out he was. Do you know what I mean, Precious?"

"Yes, Mama, I understand. Just change the locks, fire the maid and go get an HIV test." Valerie was always the practical one.

"I don't blame Magdalena. She's new to this country and there's the language barrier, and she probably was too scared to say no to him…"

"Mama, Maceo is new to this country also and doesn't speak much English either. Now he has fresh deep scratches all down his back, the kind a man gets when he makes his partner very happy, according to you, so why not 'fire' both of them and be done with it?"

© 2016 Jeanne Powell

"Hush, Valerie, don't talk about Maceo that way – he almost became your stepfather!"

At this point Valerie wanted to cry from frustration. She loved her mother and was delighted that Candy had won a small fortune in last year's Super Lotto. If only Candy could enjoy life more instead of stumbling in and out of soap opera scenarios. Did she really need an upstairs maid? Couldn't she just employ Merry Maids to send in a cleaning team once or twice a week?

"Mama, I have to go. They're expecting me at the courthouse. I have translating to do. Call me this evening if you still need to talk." Sometimes she wished she lived across the country from her mother instead of across the street.

Valerie finished her second glass of pinot noir, reapplied her pancake makeup and dashed downstairs to her gleaming Yamaha, eager for the open road.

© 2016 Jeanne Powell

Coconut Cake

Her sturdy desk is the husk of a Singer sewing machine from another century. With her back to the light flooding through dormer windows, she sits and writes, reads, dreams high above the city streets. Safe at last on the top floor of a Victorian triplex, safe from the prying eyes of covetous men and quarrelsome relatives and the unkindness of time, she ponders the lemon butter sun of a minuscule town in the Texas Panhandle.

She was 16 and her cries should have shattered the sky. Alone in the one-story house, she was absorbed in baking a coconut cake for Eduardo, her favorite uncle, due in from Austin that very evening. Silently, the widower from next door stopped by, startled her, said he was looking for her parents and had not seen them drive away in their truck. "Odd," she thought, and turned around to finish shredding coconut.

The neighbor's powerful arms threw her against the wall and lifted her into harm's way. Dazed from the attack, Missy could not fight back. Afterwards, he left her on the linoleum floor, half propped against the blue wall.

The kitchen screen door slammed and she heard the widower's leather boots crunch on dry dirt as he retreated to his house. Still later, she heard a single shotgun blast. When her parents roared up in their dusty truck, Missy still sat on the worn linoleum floor, staring into space.

© 2016 Jeanne Powell

Selected Poetry

from
February Voices
[1994]

A Poet At 79
for Libby Brahms

Gathered into wisdom
nestled
around her essence
deftly she marshals
a parliament of
memories   images
seven years of exaltation
as poet   storyteller
celebrations of a partnership
outwitting five decades
of domesticity
a singer of songs
for the daughters of Sarah
with a dancer's measured grace
gently she wears
the murmuration of years

© 2016 Jeanne Powell

FLASHBACK

The house leans with a slow creak, waiting
ladybugs slip through tears in porch screens,
    their explorations undisturbed
dust clusters solemnly under a rocking chair,
    still in its corner
worn steps stand free of smudged calling cards
generated by paws and fingers and bare feet

Dandelion greens parallel cracked sidewalks,
    reveling in their longevity
backyard clotheslines gavotte with summer breezes,
    burdened only with time
under the peach tree lie wildflowers
freshly cut, tangled, their fragrance
bleeding through fallen leaves

© 2016 Jeanne Powell

Meditation (1987-1989)

Stealthy dream-weaving threads
play hide and seek
needling vulnerable surfaces
into vivid patterns

Bleached pine cones
nestle
on a dusty dashboard

Raspberry truffles
sweeten
nocturnal bike rides

Red-splashed Chinese watercolors
adorn
a kitchen wall

Vintage port
dances
in water tumblers

Searching glances in disguise
embrace
across a noisy room

Gentle warriors
spar
with attitudes and emotions

His bright summer
softens
her autumnal fierceness

Fragile fabric
envelops images and impulses
transforming into
experience and memory

© 2016 Jeanne Powell

MADRE
for Blanche

God wasn't anywhere she had been
she never said but the children knew
even before she stored widow's weeds
and took flight at the break of dawn

Her Rosicrucian quest in the deserts of
the West was for enlightenment, she said
like Sally Hemings' Jefferson
in meditation at Bermuda Hundred

A touch of Eastern wisdom moved her
to camouflage in shawls and cowls
negating bloodsoaked memories
of Christian auction blocks

The wind brought her back one evening
from places where lilies bloomed in
soil made rich by Black-Eyed Susans
cut down in history's lurch

But she hadn't come all the way home
she never said but the children knew
oh, her gestures were there and a
placating presence in the rocking chair

Her wings were tucked so fiercely,
feathery quills pierced her flesh;
children's hands reaching, seeking,
came away stained and chilled

© 2016 Jeanne Powell

East Bay Miracle
Oakland, California 1993

Televersion
burbles
fact-based images
penetrating
mind wombs
with shotgun precision
until an implant
mushrooms
into a life term

Shot while thieving
sad-eyed woman
pregnant with failure
lingers
in dead zone limbo
pinned by surprise
three times running –
semen, bullets,
medical circus

Newspeak trumpets:
mother-to-be
dead to the world
barren of power
strapped in twilight
let go a living child
while men in white
immerse themselves
in afterbirth of glory

© 2016 Jeanne Powell

The Lazarus experts
bundle their orphan
their caesarian find
to the welfare network
on primetime schedule;
from grave to cradle
better living through
competition for the best
experiments in Black.

Memoir

Whenever plum wine permeates her brain
she reflects on an Alabama engineer
whom she abandoned on an East Bay freeway
one particularly nerve-wracking afternoon

His country pride troubled her urban stance:
honey-glazed corn bread he baked in a
    heartshaped pan
feathered creatures he gunned down (in season)
then stuffed with wild rice dressing
his prayers on Baptist knee at bedside
followed by long nights of silent sensuality

There was his martyred mother, conjured up
with wistful word portraits of her
    gnarled fingers
poring over well-thumbed scriptures,
her meditations split apart by his
    axe-wielding father
on a midnight chase through stubbled fields

Engineering is a science, he was taught
building bridges is an art she learned
but everything came tumbling down
one particularly nerve-wracking afternoon

© 2016 Jeanne Powell

Games

Honest enemies she likes best
they deliver calling cards before
    dispatching assassins
she's ready then for the cut and slash,
    hit and run
or at least she's not surprised.

but those others,
the ones who chat her up
and invite confidences over
    croissants and cappuccino,
who want to get to KNOW her
    – she's so different –
THEY sniff and poke,
    wheedle and implore
to satisfy their curiosity.

beneath her clever parries
they detect pain
    – oh! how boring –
and away they glide
in search of other
amusements.

© 2016 Jeanne Powell

DAMAGE CONTROL
on being friends with liberals

They said they wanted to be my friends
With rose petal tones and hard, bright smiles
Scarred talons gripped as they paraded me about
Another prized acquisition from a ghetto fire sale

Like a biblical scourge, they attacked without cause
Arrayed in the chain mail of hereditary masters
In their fists gleamed knives dipped in gossip and rumor
Their palms shimmered with Bantu heads on silver coins

Lashing out, they wandered off, guilt-ridden Janus ghosts
Masturbating on dying cacti in nocturnal Berkeley gardens
"We bleed too, so anything we do to you is justified"
And slumping into Aryan dung with Arkansas smiles

© 2016 Jeanne Powell

DEMPSEY

Summer days whenever the wind was under wraps
Dempsey – if he claimed another name no one knew –
sat in a chair for sale under the lone leafy tree
near the curb and visited with the sun
presiding over the little shop
all the time sundry shoppers
were looking after him on the sly

even if he hadn't said he had seen it all
they would've known from his weather-beaten grin
and leathery voice as he selected favorites among
the seasoned strollers for barter and swap of tales
and gems of another kind the moment new faces
fit into old places in his mind's eye

breathless and dark-eyed a part-time gypsy
entered laughing with earrings dancing and
focused in time on this wizened barnacle
of a mariner/iron monger/gandy dancer
who left his chair with difficulty now but
whose eyes followed as she floated through
the curio shop searching for pewter bowls
copper kettles and silver demitasse spoons

hearing out Dempsey's word tapestries of worldwide
travel was what most shoppers did those lingering
summer afternoons except she really listened
encircling him with gentle quips and queries
waiting to view treasures he'd held back for
her eyes alone—miniature cups from dusty shelves
fairy tales in leather binding and silver demitasse spoons

© 2016 Jeanne Powell

where've you been, Demitasse? wistful query and reproach
when journeys of the mind kept her away too long from
Dempsey's failing sight and riveting tales of how it was
a full half century ago as Pennsylvania steel drivers
and coal miners fought the bosses and she wondered
whose bright image her presence called to mind
from that time of solidarity in rainbow hues

so continued their dialogue laced with merry exchanges
and memories come alive until one winddriven afternoon
the shop overflowed with empty chairs and a handwritten sign
shouted through the window Dempsey died in the night
his heart attacked without warning and he couldn't rally—
still, she visited the shop from time to time
perching on chairs for sale and glancing about
then whispering goodbye and trudging down the city hill

© 2016 Jeanne Powell

Summer School 1991

Tina with wise, world-weary eyes
and satin skin of burnished brown
whose swinging hips and brittle laugh
resound when she walks "like the ladies do"

Tina now still and so remote
fragile face enameled in pain
at the touch of memories
not meant for six-year-olds

Tina who drew a solitary flower
a pulsing heart in red crayon
the bluest sky with granite clouds
Tina whose courage teaches daily

how do I bring out the sun for you?

© 2016 Jeanne Powell

TRIAGE

> *I Remember Nothing More*
> *(The Warsaw Children's Hospital*
> *and the Jewish Resistance)*
> —Adina Blady Szwajger, M.D.

What emotions devoured your thoughts
that sundrenched afternoon
the enemy is coming, tearing through lifetimes
young you were, to be so burdened
how did you steel yourself
still the shaking tray
fill the hypodermics that cloudless day
the enemy is coming, burning up memories
did they smile, the children
in hospital pallets' ragged rows
as you attended one last time
the enemy is coming, crushing defenses

fiercely you loved them
your tiny charges, and stood as parent
doing what only a parent could do
      must
            do
the enemy is coming, slicing through reason
to transport your patients, the children
your children now, to their new home
in a special camp where dreams are butchered
gently you placed the hypodermics
injecting dosages lethal
protecting for all time as many as you could
the enemy is coming, piercing through hope
and suffer the little children must not

© 2016 Jeanne Powell

Winnie Mandela

What are the duties of a wife
when her husband fights in prison
and her children plead for life?

What are the duties of a woman
when her home lies in ashes
and police rape her sisters?

What are the duties of a patriot
when young students are teargassed
and Steve Biko is martyred?

What are the duties of a warrior
when her nation chokes in bondage
and her people cry for justice?

What are the duties of a chieftain –
to dance in the quicksand of Western acclaim
or to clothe herself in the fury of the fallen?

Must her battle tactics at the barricades
be pedestal-pure during all those years
when her cause was survival itself?

© 2016 Jeanne Powell

Neighbors

Draped in unrepentant purple,
husband and suitcases trailing,
she strolled through our courtyard
sidestepping little corpses
heading straight as the crow flies
for her rustic cabin refuge buried deep
in scruffy shrubs near Bodega Bay

Word flies fast among winged brethren,
of pigeon eggs spooned to breaking point
on courtyard cement, of pigeon mothers
bludgeoned with Oxford dictionaries
or forked to distraction by hostile
flatware guarding embattled window boxes

It may be wise, dear neighbor to be wary
of whiskey-laden sojourns through mildewed
woods on fog-filled nights, of rural frolics
with scattered runes and buttered scones,
for feathered friends of mama pigeons
may lurk on leafy tree limbs
just   killing   time....

© 2016 Jeanne Powell

Night Crawlers
North Beach nightclub,
after hours, circa 1985

Love is a hurting thing
love can be a killer
Jocko and Parisienne
locked in intimate combat
playing love's old sweet song
on top of that roving Steinway
that took them higher and higher

Parisienne saw the light
before she hit the ceiling
slid off Jocko and the Steinway
but Jocko was unlucky at love
for him the climax wasn't that
"little death" the French refer to
but the BIG ONE

© 2016 Jeanne Powell

© 2016 Jeanne Powell

© 2016 Jeanne Powell

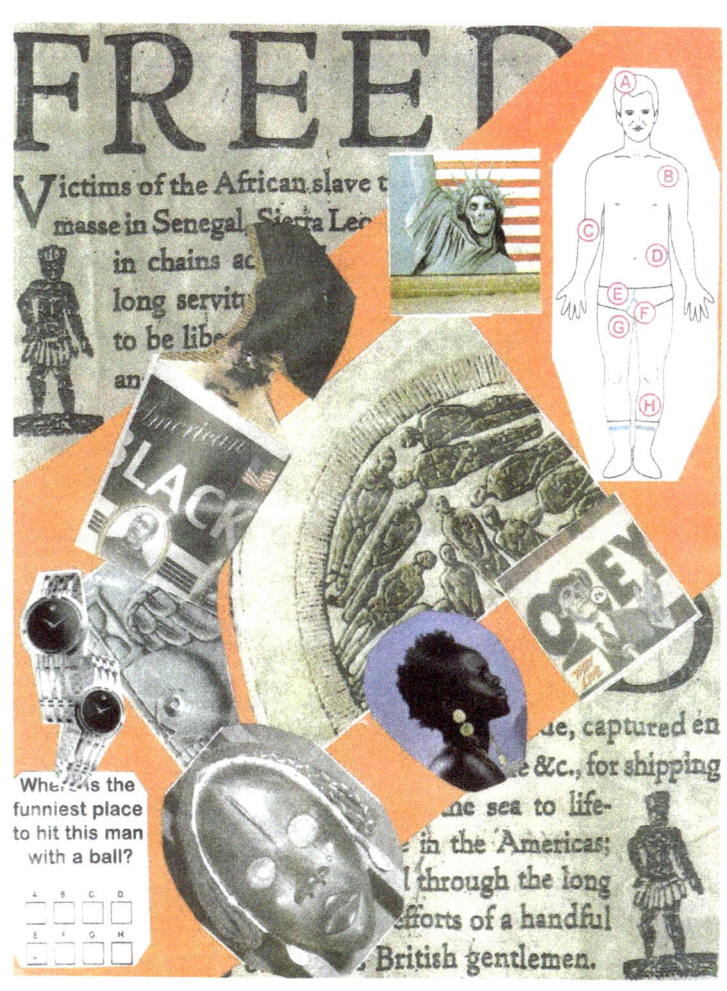

© 2016 Jeanne Powell

© 2016 Jeanne Powell

from
Cadences
[1996]

Affirmation

Poetry – the motion
I live when I walk
with bolder words

rhythm to my rhyme
as I chant through
walls of rain

the sweetness
of plum wine when
you worshipped me

wild melodies
I saved for you
before you could play

soft lyrics
you wrote for me
before I could hear

images cling
magnetized
to an iron will

crying without words
my sisters
cleave unto me

a trio of
angel voices in
canary-sweetened tunnels

poetry –
come dance with me
celebrate my life

© 2016 Jeanne Powell

Autumn Revisited

Spring embryo
summer foetus
cabernet child of autumn
never more daring
than in fall
when ripe red
cascades into orange and gold
yellow and amber, shading
softly to sweet cinnamon brown.
Born in
Cheyenne Cherokee Chippewa summer
guarded by the Mistress of poets
in autumn veils,
such a child
would edit
an earthly master

  ★

It's hard
to be
fall…
the work of extinguishing the world…
a job
for strong hands.
  Sí pero
One woman to another
I've always wanted
to be fall's apprentice
a younger sister.

© 2016 Jeanne Powell

★

It's hard,
this long drawn-out work of ours.
We've got to
ready the earth...
    Sí pero
We help Her shelter the seeds
that will sleep
in Her womb, guarded
by two red horsewomen
who run around the world:
autumn's apprentice
and autumn herself.

I was born
knowing autumn, knowing
how to mother the earth.

Inspired by *Oda al otoño* by Pablo Neruda

© 2016 Jeanne Powell

Experiencing Technical Difficulties

Hear the story never-ending   barefoot gazelle
mountain ewe, rainforest cheetah who ran for her life
a life any life   like the wind against the wind
whose life is it anyway   where the runner stumbles
and the lady is for burning   three blazing strikes
in a firestorm of foul play   stormy weather
on a clear day she could have seen forever could have
written the funniest play you ever read   did
you hear her calling you out to play, to bear witness,
do you see what she saw   she was alive then
did you bury her truth under the bluest sky with
granite clouds   when a single flower in red
crayon stood for something   a final stand   a
lasting impression of her mind dangling   a rope
twisting in the wind-break   she fell such a long
way   can you hear her calling about the tear in time's
fabric   asking for a stitch in time   to save a
life for the giving   in season and out there is
the truth   is anyone hearing   is anyone there

© 2016 Jeanne Powell

In the Shadow of the Bridge
(Thanksgiving Day 1995)

The little girl who lives in apartment 20A
in the shadow, in the shadow of Manhattan Bridge
she died last night – no one could spare
the courage to give her one more year

her cries and screams through neighboring walls
"Please, Mommy, I'm sorry!" pleading for time
time to soothe and relieve the mysterious rage
of a renegade mother, or gentleman caller
              yet unnamed

tearful in handcuffs, the benighted mother
led away to dance with criminal justice
pleads no knowledge of her daughter's cries
for reprieve, time to hope, on Thanksgiving eve

contrite neighbors later hang their heads
parade before the camera's piercing eye
their lack of haste in summoning police
laid to waste Alisa, an unquiet death

sweet of face, greatly bruised in heart and limb
her long hair soaked in maternal rage, let down
let down one last time, Alisa, in a tiny shroud
in the shadow, in the shadow of the Bridge

© 2016 Jeanne Powell

January—In the Rain
(a monologue)

Get up, get up, old man
from that bed of roses
where you're trying to be sick

don't you die on me
you son-of-a-bitch
or I'll kill you for spite

can't be seen at the city morgue
have no time to plot your wake
not in any attitude I own

grieving about your sorry life
doesn't fit my shopping list
the blues-basket is full enough

children fired up my house
burned away my rose-colored dreams
now I've got to fly away home

you want time I can't supply
time that's mortgaged and long gone
let your debts try to keep you warm

get on up before the cops pounce
before those thorns cut through
your bag of bones and "should've-been" woes

don't you die on me
you son-of-a-bitch
'cause I'll kill you for spite

© 2016 Jeanne Powell

Journey

The moment my soles touched the tarmac
I did not think of you at all   the old gang
enveloped me in sweet-tasting tavern songs
and marching chants, evoking times when walls
tumbled and dreams lived hard but high up where
all could see and gain the heart they had to have

in honor of my visit we would mourn Plum Street
conjure Canada outlaws,
celebrate Greektown excursions,
recall car treks to Nine Mile Drive along
rock salted lanes to view Christmas miracles
in the snow   I did not think of you at all

at times a traffic signal took too long to change
and I would see your face in profile on an iced-over
sign warning of washed-out roads or detours just ahead
then friends would turn our car into an evergreen drive
where warmer faces waited to rekindle select days
as is proper on a journey of the heart

once under the weeping willow in Louise's back yard
I thought I saw a wedge from a croquet mallet, faded
paint blending into winter grass barely exposed
but from the porch came shouts reassuring in their
heartiness that hot mulled wine was waiting and so
there was no time to think of you at all

© 2016 Jeanne Powell

Running Wild

Twilight hours when night and day
have their brief encounter
she likes to lope along the boulevards
circulating in her territorial way
sees him without looking at first
imprisoned still
in her merely human form
wide gait eating up the concrete
her eyes arc side to side
softly brushing his wolfen
presence with her spirit
before she really knows him

magnificence black and silver
canine lupus on an urban visit
owning the front seat of that
     Ford pickup
his human pets nearby
golden eyes seek hers
their spirits lock
he is beside her on the pavement
timeless wild face raised in fierce
     silence   he KNOWS her
twilight when worlds open and brush
bittersweet intercourse
tantalizing in its fleeting touch

© 2016 Jeanne Powell

smothering oaths, his human handlers
 spring to grasp
the collar around his massive neck
struggling to return him to their
 small world
reclaimed by her neon desert
she ponders the beauty of him
 that moment together
considers backtracking to pick up
 the scent
rip out the throats of his jailers
then sighs and inhales slowly
loping through time

Souvenirs

My anger
you have not seen
yet always you say
when we recall
the First Americans
you feel its sharp edge
drawing blood
souvenirs to hone
the memories

conquistadores
branded Chiricahua hearts
seared Mescalero souls
left chilling images
in desert graves
calling cards of
the Grand Inquisitor
in the name of
civilization

Cherokee, Choctaw
before their Trail of Tears
Chickasaw, Creek
fought back in Christian clothes
fortress dwellers bleeding time
death chants rose above the flames
hot tribal juices trickled down
potato harvest was stored below
a tasty meal by all accounts

© 2016 Jeanne Powell

young mothers' brown breasts
made soft tobacco pouches
button makers' eastern skills
enlivened confiscated bones
a fallen chief's heroic head
pickled in wine, spiced up
the talk at the general store
among sacks of flour and
barrels of nails

Powder River, Sand Creek
if the Long Death had ended there
Little Big Horn, Wounded Knee
you could acknowledge the cost
three generations since, and more
medical doctors through fraud and deceit
robbed Reservation women of their eggs
cut their tubes without consent
the Holocaust begins again

my anger
you have not seen
yet always you say
when we recall
the First Americans
you feel its sharp edge
drawing blood
think of those drops
as souvenirs

© 2016 Jeanne Powell

Street Music

We paused in our walk, our conversation, talking
women   poetry   spirituality
waiting for traffic signals to glow
another color   our hearts circulating
women's poetry and women's art
through mind and soul, barely attuned
to nightdriven sound and alien shadows –
and heard a rhapsody in street rhyme

we paused in our talk, our exploration, quoting
poetry   women   sensuality
waiting for a light to change its direction –
and heard a rhapsody in street rhyme.
Attentive peers encircled a corner rapper
his words slamming forth in a fusillade.
Reassuring my wary friend, I stopped
to hear more of the pattern and the power,
this proud young poet exploding phrases
in a corner of our world

here's another poet   let's listen
but she concentrated on the light ahead,
responding to its predictable change.
Fragile profile poised for flight,
my friend would not be reassured.
Listen   he's a poet too don't you hear
but she would not turn, could not see,
did not feel his rhapsody in street rhyme

© 2016 Jeanne Powell

I remembered then too many evenings
when a young male voice raised in anger
in the street anywhere   any year
meant uncertainty   caution   danger   fear
for women rich in the artistry of life.
It's all right   he's a singer of songs
like you and me, shall we listen

but the signal beckoned and this time
we crossed to safer ground.
The rhapsody in street rhyme,
a corner wordsmith's vivid challenge –
haunted, echoed as we passed

© 2016 Jeanne Powell

from
Tangerine Dance
[1999]

The Assassin

Bay windows shimmer where he stands
on a picture perfect afternoon
framed in flashpoints of sunlight he is
desperately in search of cover

across the living room she glowed
exulted in his safe return however unsteady
his direction   back in the world   walking point
from kitchen to backyard barbecue

thick carpet   forest green   obliterates
their teakwood floor   disguises her barefoot steps
as she glides through the rainforest
blanketed in pink-foamed mist

she peers around rubber trees charred and leaking
slips closer to the man's shadow at bay
this picture perfect afternoon
smiling with the innocence of a

wife whose home has never been napalmed
the woman pads softly past a bamboo table
with its porcelain vase of bougainvillea
through the rice paddies flooding the carpet

deep in country now the man feels her
reaching across   and turns just in time
to rescue her from friendly fire   his face
a Magritte landscape in disarray

© 2016 Jeanne Powell

Tangerine

Yesterday
just before sunset
you asked me to peel a tangerine
without bruising its sweet flesh
take off the skin in pieces
you said   the way I do it

what you did not say
remember how I sectioned your carapace
tease-peeled your boundaries
one chambered hope at a time
down to the nerve-crammed raw
until the flesh crimsoned and

tiny blood blossoms – startled –
desperate to cover the loss
spread their untried petals
looking for a miracle
to stem the flow   salvage
a sense of self

see   like this
you gestured   smiling
a saucer of tart segments
pared and dripping
my skinless face reflected
in the juices puddled at the edge

© 2016 Jeanne Powell

Saint Thomas on Hyde Street

Discreetly past the midnight hour
sweet Thomas ascends the winding stairs
each well trodden step a tortuous one
with fluttering heart and lacerated palm
he beats beats beats on the door

The neighborly man in leather
sends a German to the weathered door
behind her the others array themselves
we're going to bed now she says
there will be no noise tonight

He returns to his room comatose
high heeled leather   dancing boots
ricochet through the depths of his despair
a knife in his hand a din in his head
a clown driven mad by a merry-go-round

© 2016 Jeanne Powell

Seeing Miss Rosa (1997)

Two women boarded the same city bus
one at a time   on different streets   from separate worlds
a generation   and two lifetimes apart

Purposeful and unbent, the brown-eyed traveler
boarded, searched and sat   still more wary than careworn
close enough to the front of the bus to honor Rosa Parks
and vindicate her own life for a moment or two

Confident and rigid, the blue-eyed commuter
entered, perused and stood   still more certain than sentient
close enough to the other's seat to validate the perception
that her need ruled

I see said the brown-eyed visage
so that is how it is with you still
I know said the blue-eyed masque
what has always been mine

Yes said the brown-eyed soul   I see
that you wait and you will wait forever   for we need
the Rules to be the same for both of us and I shall
not be moved by your Need alone

A gentle lady stood up once so that I might sit down today –
you need to sit down and think about the rules which render me
invisible to you   you need to sit down and think
but not here and not now!

© 2016 Jeanne Powell

Keeping Watch

History selects the heroines
we immortalize in story and song
victors promote their profiles
on coins of the realm, each carrying
her weight with stoic grace
leaving us with feelings we can endure

To make it real, though, for it to matter
deep within that we are here, we need to
stand in the rain, candles lit and covered,
by the centuries of unmarked graves
the nameless maidens, mothers, crones
buried alive for the practice of female wiles

The fugitive slave, breast milk leaking,
bare fists striking at the bounty hunters
fell to Earth's sweet scented grass bereft
of sound while badges of her courage
flowed everywhere that summer's day
remember her

Fannie Lou Hamer whose body grew thick
from backroom blows delivered under color of
authority why couldn't she stay in her place
she sobbed from the punishing challenge of not
recalling her place they beat her because
she remembered to stand

© 2016 Jeanne Powell

Named for the angels the quiet teacher who
breathed Marx and Engels the way we take in air
dragged from her innocence in chains
if they come for her in the morning
they will come for me at night
if you fail to stand and remember

Hold the memories of their bones and blood
know the way to the underground stations still
keep watch by the rivers and the streams
like the warrior that you are, bear witness
in the rain, candles lit and covered, for we need to
stand and remember

Voyager raindrops
playfully birdtracking each
well traveled window

Organic love free
of all known toxicity
except the wanting

© 2016 Jeanne Powell

Main street sidewalk grief
iridescent plumage down
death of a hummingbird

Life experience
you can take it to the bank
not   easy   money!

Seasoned countenance
final journey in this life
coriander bliss

I have seen the mayor
five times since the election
still no proposal

Mad Milosevic
suicide claimed his parents
were they his first kill?

Brazen mulberries
tantalize my midnight soul
wild dreamtime dancing

I Looked for You in a Mayonnaise Jar

When those furry little raindrops
scurried through the open window
scooted
        down
                my
                        fevered
                                cheeks
I knew
you were gone
the mayonnaise jar prone and empty
glistening from your Burma Shave
handprints, discarded without a trace
of residue or remorse,
like the last seven years of my life

        TO BE CONTINUED...

        © 2016 Jeanne Powell

A Trace of Honey
(for F.C.)

I have been angry all week she frets
a trace of honey in her puzzled voice
cultured pearls whipping along
her town and country dress

He's been gone since January
and it has been really great   though
not even El Niño can erase 30 years
of bitter harvest in wildflower country

On the back of her painted filly
she rides out the storms
jumping over beehives and hurdles
which toppled less perfect unions

Striding through her garden full
of morning glory and hardy roses
she hums as the telephone rings
the sound of her sons' voices

sweet harvest honeycombing
every   newborn   day

© 2016 Jeanne Powell

The Shadow Knows

I used to spend all my time
trying to get ahead
now I plot to get a leg
up on time
an arm around its
relentless shadow
seeping
flowing
marching
beyond all memories
borne and unborn
toward a once and future calm

© 2016 Jeanne Powell

 ## *About Jeanne Powell*

Published poet and cultural critic.

Author of flash fiction and film reviews.

Eternal word dancer.

http://jeanne-powell.com

www.ingramcontent.com/pod-product-compliance
Lightning Source LLC
Chambersburg PA
CBHW040322300426
44112CB00020B/2839